I0201522

I Am Not
To Be Sold!

I AM NOT TO BE SOLD!

(A Human trafficking Anthology)

origami

Parrésia Publishers Ltd.
23, Opebi road, Ikeja, Lagos, Nigeria.
+2348154582178, +2348062392145
parresia@parresia.com.ng
www.parresia.com.ng/origami

Copyright © 2016
The right of Tobore Ighofume Ovuorie to be identified as the editor of this work has been
asserted by her in accordance with the copyright Law of the Federal Republic of Nigeria.

All rights reserved. Other than brief excerpts for reviews and commentaries, no part of this
publication may be produced, stored in a retrieval system or transmitted in any for or by
any means, electronic, mechanical, photocopying, recording or otherwise, without the prior
permission of the Publisher.

ISBN: 978-978-85407-9-76

Printed in Nigeria by Parrésia Press

For trafficked and abused children all over the world.

WOUNDED GIRL

May wounds such as mine
Drive lunacy off men's minds
I pray God if you still care
For kids like I who are so scared

Tobore Ovuorie,
Senior Secondary School 1,
June 1995,
14 years old.

CONTENTS

Dedication 5

Introduction 9

1.   A Treacherous World 11
2.   Why Must I Be Sold? 12
3.   I Am Not An Item 13
4.   I Am The Apple Of God's Eyes 14
5.   I Am Born Free 15
6.   Neo-Colonialism Of Africans By Africans 16
7.   I Am Priceless! 17
8.   No Currency Can Buy Me! 18
9.   Grateful To Modern Slavery 19
10. Countless Rands Not Worth Your Dignity! 21
11. Was Obama Sold? 22
12. Parents Why Sell Your Children? 23
13. Come Rain Come Sunshine 24
14. My Heart Bleeds 25
15. I Am Born To Be Free 26
16. I Am An Asset To This Society 27
17. Slavery Is Death Of The Soul 28
18. Too Precious To Be Priced! 29
19. Did I Hear You Rain Curses On Traffickers? 30

Index of Poets 31

INTRODUCTION

Media Initiative Against Human Trafficking and Women Rights Abuse (MIAHWRA) is a non-profit, non-denominational and non-partisan organisation founded in August 2015. We centre our efforts on preventing and eliminating the trafficking of individuals and dealing with the abuse of women and girls from a human rights and gender-based approach.

I Am Not To Be Sold is the fruit of MIAHWRA's maiden project, which entailed moving from school-to-school (S2S) to educate students about human trafficking. Weeks before our awareness creation sessions in 2015, we had requested that the children write poems on the theme "I Am Not To Be Sold". Some of the children were given prizes for their effort. Particularly, the director of Mafazat Comprehensive High School, Alagbado, Lagos, awarded scholarships to six students for their outstanding performance in our competition.

Sadly, on the 15th April, 2016, another young lady very dear to MIAHWRA was trafficked to Italy. It dawned on us that we needed to multiply our efforts at reaching out to the youths which was when the idea of publishing *I Am Not To Be Sold* popped up.

In our poetry reservoir are over two hundred poems by secondary school students who have taken part in the MIAHWRA Human Trafficking Awareness Competition. Only a few of these poems have made it into this human trafficking anthology for fiscal reasons. We would, however, be giving secondary school students copies of the books for free in our S2S awareness creation programmes. This, we believe, will not only create the intended orientation in that vulnerable demographic but also inspire them to write honest literary pieces, as they would be groomed on how to write short stories from scratch through our various literary workshops. Outstanding work would then be published in our 2017 short stories collection.

It is our dream at MIAHWRA that every Nigerian child gets a copy of this book. It is our ambition to destroy the human trafficking trade, thereby making the world safer for everyone, particularly women and children.

Tobore Ovuorie,
Founder/Executive Director

A TREACHEROUS WORLD

By

Jibreel A.M. Moshood

A shameful and worthless act in this world we live today
Surely a literate mind can clearly see the truth without obscurity
Slavery is very much alive and gets strengthened each dawn of a new day
A mortal sin attacking the vital tenets within us all

Vulnerable young women exploited and forced into all sorts of hard labour
Working steadfastly in extreme heat and as sex slaves at dusk of every new day
Sometimes get sold off at very ridiculous prices
And accused of all sorts of evil vices, then disgraced and shamed

Avalanches of tears roll down my sorrow bedraggled eyes
When I reminisce about the sufferings of the so-called slaves
I soliloquize about the so-called human rights activists
And I ask myself do they really worth to be called that?

A lot of families have been torn apart
Thanks to the gruesome touch of greed
The so-called masters of slavery project something they are not to the outside
    world
Whereas at the other dark end lies their evil secrets.

*Jibreel A.M. Moshood is a Senior Secondary School 3 student and this poem, written
in November 2015, won the Senior Category, MIAHWRA Human Trafficking
Awareness Competition For Secondary School Students.*

WHY MUST I BE SOLD?

By

John Teslim Raphael

I am not to be sold
The words of pain coming from Africans
The agony in our voices speaks the truth
Why am I to be sold?
I am the beauty of the world

I am not to be sold
Because I am made of flesh and blood
I am not to be sold
Because integrity lies in me

All in this world witness day and night
Both black and white
Then why am I to be sold?

I am not to be sold
Because God has created me in His image
I am not to be sold because
I am one whole generation
I am not to be sold because
Generations after me are going to be
The face of the earth
Then tell me, why must I be sold?

John Teslim Raphael is a Senior Secondary School 2 student. He wrote this poem in November 2015 and was a finalist in the Senior Category, MIAHWRA Human Trafficking Awareness Competition For Secondary School Students.

I AM NOT AN ITEM!

By

Abass. O. Mistura

I am born free
Beautifully created by Almighty God
And He has given me freedom
So why would one else want to seize it?

I Abass Oyinkansola Mistura refuse to be sold
I can never be sold because of luxuries, cars, houses
Or wealth that won't last long
Then I lose my respect
Lose my integrity and all is wasted

I am not a slave
I am not anyone's servant
I am not an item anyone can pass around
Because I want luxuries will I now become a prostitute?
NEVER!

I refuse to be sold
I am great on my own
I am great the way I am
Almighty God created me for a purpose
He gave me life, so why would one else seize it?

I am not an item
I refuse to be sold
I can never be sold
I am not to be sold
I am born free.

Abass O. Mistura is a Senior Secondary School 2 student. She wrote this poem in November 2015 and was a finalist in the Senior Category, MIAHWRA Human Trafficking Awareness Competition For Secondary School Students.

I AM THE APPLE OF GOD'S EYES

By

Folarin Oreoluwa

I am the apple of God's eyes
I was created by the greatest artist to look nice
And nurtured by my parents to be intelligent and wise
I am the boundless cool wind that blows
I am that diamond glints on snow
And I will surely glow

I am the sunlight on ripened grain
I am the gentle autumn rain
These are unquantifiable and unsellable
So you see, I am not to be sold
But should and will rule the world and reign
Instead of being sold for money without gain.

Folarin Oreoluwa is a Junior Secondary School 1 student and this poem, written in November 2015, won the Junior Category, MIAHWRA Human Trafficking Awareness Competition For Secondary School Students.

I AM BORN FREE!

By

Oyedele Habibat

Allah has given me soul
And He said *inna alabarika fiha amodan*
Everyone is equal before Almighty Allah
I am born a free person

Why must I be sold to a fellow human being?
I refuse to be sold
If you want to be sold, choose you so
But I refuse to be sold in exchange for anything

When I die, will I be buried with wealth in the grave?
So I say NO to selling me
I will keep my dignity
I am worth far more than precious stones!

Oyedele Habibat is a Junior Secondary School 3 student. She wrote this poem in November 2015 and was a finalist in the Junior Category, MIAHWRA Human Trafficking Awareness Competition For Secondary School Students.

NEO-COLONIALISM OF AFRICANS BY AFRICANS

By

Abd'raheem Abd'rahman

My forefathers were taken as slaves
With their lips sealed with iron, working on farms of white imperialists
Why should I allow history repeat itself?
By searching for needless greener pasture
A pasture that is a real prison
Working without pay
Sweating to fill the purse of some greedy nuisance

I will not be drawn into this neocolonialism
Inflicted on Africans by Africans
Teenagers working as sex slaves
Degrading the beautiful African culture of abstinence
I will not leave my fatherland
Rich beauty of the smiling sun and rainbows
For shameful toils like a cheap toy.

Abd'raheem Abd'rahman is a Junior Secondary School 3 student. He wrote this poem in November 2015 and was a finalist in the Junior Category, MIAHWRA Human Trafficking Awareness Competition For Secondary School Students.

I AM PRICELESS!

By

Tijani Rahmat Morenikeji

What I heard wasn't just a voice
It gets louder and louder
I ponder and wonder
What could it be?
What could it mean?

You are not to be sold nor borrowed
You are an earthling with a concept
An individual with a prospect
It said

Now, sitting and thinking
Laying and imagining
Truly I am not to be sold
In me, I have hidden promises to fulfill

Why should I be sold?
Why should I?

I am too worthy to be sold
I am extraordinary
I am priceless
My existence is a beautiful treasure

The voice at peace
In stillness it speaks
As a reminder and warning
You are not to be sold.

Tijani Rahmat Morenikeji is a Senior Secondary School 3 student. She wrote this poem on November 22nd, 2015.

NO CURRENCY CAN BUY ME!

By

Odunlami Faruq

I am a precious stone
More than the diamond that glitters
Which is worth a fair fortune
And is always cherished

I am not to be sold
Cause I am worth more than gold
I am an egg to the world
No currency can buy me

I have great missions
That must be achieved
And surely I will
No heartless soul can stop me

Odunlami Faruq *wrote this poem in November 2015.*

GRATEFUL TO MODERN SLAVERY

By

Ettu-Ekundayo Monsurat

Pain hits my heart
Sorrow sleeps in my mind
As I watch our lives get ruined
By some strangers and leaders
Enslaving us for their own future
Making us undergo torture

Tears at full speed
Run from the corner of my brain
To my eyes down to my cheeks
Fighting to get its freedom

How I wish
I only wish
We could pick up our guns and swords
To fight back at them
To stand up for ourselves
Against pain and sorrow

They are irresponsible
They aid in our ill fate of slavery
But we seem not ready
For freedom and truth

Embracing their ways
As our way of life
Neglecting the ways of our ancestors
Ingrates we are to the old paths of our culture
Grateful to modern slavery
Such a tedious tale of foolery!

Not until we learn to follow our own ways
Not until we embrace our culture
Not until we appreciate our rich tradition
Shall we be free from the bond of modern slavery

Ettu-Ekundayo Monsurat *is a Senior Secondary School 3 student. She wrote this poem on November 22nd, 2015.*

COUNTLESS RANDS NOT WORTH YOUR DIGNITY!

By

Ogunsola Mariam

Your life has no currency
Countless rands are not worth your dignity
Pricing your body cannot give you identity
Avoid affinity
And lift your integrity

Human-figured minds
Myopic about immoral lives
Why can't they just move away from these shattered lives?

Humans treated as objects in exchange for a decent life
Ripping away dreams, shattering lives

Their hearts are stone cold
Even while they grow old
Drenched with much hatred
Even to their toes
Yet the truth remains untold

This is a new generation
With less integration
And no future intention

God owns your soul
Remember someday He will call you home
What He gave you shouldn't be sold
You are not your own.

Ogunsola Mariam is a Senior Secondary School 3 student. She wrote this poem in November 2015.

WAS OBAMA SOLD?

By

Balogun Khadijah

I am not to be slaved
I am a world-class being
I am tomorrow's person of power

Muhammadu Buhari was not sold
Or he wouldn't have become Nigeria's president
Or was he sold?

Babatunde Raji Fashola was not sold
If not, he wouldn't be a global reference point in leadership
Or should he have been sold?

America's Barack Obama was not sold
Was Obama sold, really?
So how did he become President of the United States?

My future is brighter than even theirs
Lay not your filthy hands on me
I am the much anticipated Change

Balogun Khadijah *is a Senior Secondary School 3 student. She wrote this poem in November 2015.*

PARENTS, WHY SELL YOUR CHILDREN?

By

Tijani Saheed

We are all equal in the presence of God
So I must not be sold
Parents, why sell your children?
Is it for money, earthly materials and fame?
Quit selling what you can't create
Don't you know they are tomorrow's leaders?

I hear you say it's because of poverty
I also hear unemployment
Did you create the air you breathe?
Can you sell the air you inhale?
Then why sell kids you can't create?

Children are immeasurably unsellable
We are not to be sold

Tijani Saheed *is a Senior Secondary School 1 student. He wrote this poem in November 2015.*

COME RAIN COME SUNSHINE

By

Lamidi Kafilat

My dignity is my pride
Whoever sells his or her dignity has lost all
Come rain, come sunshine
I will keep mine

Even if it warrants me
Losing the last drop of my blood
I choose never to sell myself
I pray for God's guidance

I don't care if I die in the cause of poverty
I choose to face such life's calamities
Than place myself up for sale
Come rain, come sunshine

God said He created all of us equal
Not for some to be enslaved by others

Lamidi Kafilat *is a Junior Secondary School 2 student. She wrote this poem in November 2015.*

MY HEART BLEEDS

By

John Fatiq

My heart bleeds when I see
Children my age suffering
My heart pauses every time
I see a child hawking wares
I become sad when I imagine
That a child has been trafficked

God created us for a reason
Certainly not slavery
Why should we be sold?
Our nation needs us
Slavery must be stopped
Souls must not be sold

Should I be sold for wealth?
Never!

John Fatiq is a Junior Secondary School 1 student. He wrote this poem in November 2015.

I AM BORN TO BE FREE

By

Olayanju Roqeebah

I am not to be sold
Because I am born to be free
No matter the sex, tribe or colour
I am a free girl

Being a slave doesn't befit
A healthy and productive girl like me
I am born to uplift the glory of my country
Not to be enslaved

I am entitled to a sound education
Healthcare and good living
Not to be chained like a dog
I am born to be free

I am not to be sold for any reason
As a sex tool while pimps enjoy the outcome
I am a free girl with free mind and free will
To live a self-fulfilling life

It is better to be poor than be a slave
A slave's life is not safe
Slaves are subjected to destructive inhuman conditions
I am born to be free, not to be sold

Olayanju Roqeebah is a Junior Secondary School 1 student. She wrote this poem in November 2015.

I AM AN ASSET TO THIS SOCIETY

By

Abdul-Azeez Toheeb

I am the hope of Nigeria
My light shines brightly
I am a being, not a thing
So I must never be sold

I am a success in the society
I am the medicine to your anxiety
I am the solution to Nigeria's problems
You see, I shouldn't be sold

My beauty is unknown just as are my wisdom and honour
I am a man of worth
I am an asset to this society
Only a sick mind would want to sell me!

Abdul-Azeez Toheeb is a Junior Secondary School 1 student. He wrote this poem in November 2015.

SLAVERY IS DEATH OF THE SOUL

By

Abdulsalam Muyibat

I am a creation of God
He perfectly moulded me
Not only to be free
But to be successful

I am not created for slavery
Neither for this brand of poverty
Who will save us?
Who will destroy slavery?

Poverty isn't a lack of money but death of ideas
Selling fellow humans is no idea
Slavery is death of the soul, mind and body

Abdulsalam Muyibat *is a Junior Secondary School 1 student. She wrote this poem in November 2015.*

TOO PRECIOUS TO BE PRICED!

By

Adeniyi Sekinat

You who sells people to make money
Buy cars and for popularity
And you that buys them for whatever purpose
Would the houses, cars, jewelries and luxury
You obtain follow you into the grave?

You seller and buyer
When you sell people, how do you feel?
Don't you know you're the source of others' tears?
Or you heartlessly don't care?

Had you been sold
Will you think of doing same today?
This buying fellow human beings for whatever purpose
Don't you know karma will serve you too?
Or you are living for just today?

Oh you who labours to flee to Europe
Or just any country other than here
Why do you hate yourself this much?
Oh! I'm judging you?
Then why go there for prostitution or other illegal purposes?

Why choose to waste your life?
Why heed to that which is useless?
And lose your dignity?
Or is the word pride missing from your dictionary?
Humans are too precious to be priced!

Adeniyi Sekinat is a Senior Secondary School 2 student. She wrote this poem in November 2015.

DID I HEAR YOU RAIN CURSES ON TRAFFICKERS?

By

Busari Shukrah

Lurking around embassies in our imaginations
We visit their countries in our discussions
Until the two birth reality
Even when we have no business being in such society

At dawn we curse the Naira
At dusk we blame the Dollar
Always we worship anyone living abroad
And define them as successful

We work overseas as street sweepers
Even as toilet cleaners
Hawk as club strippers
Thinking we are reapers of wealth

Traffickers latch onto our travel desperation
Enslaving us through promises of football clubs overseas
And making prostitutes of our female footballers

Did I hear you rain curses on traffickers?
We are to blame also
Don't you think so?
Ok, say a big thank you to our whack definition of success!

Busari Shukrah is a Senior Secondary School 1 student. She wrote this poem in November 2015.

INDEX OF POETS

1. Jibreel A.M Moshood
2. John Teslim Raphael
3. Abass O. Mistura
4. Folarin Oreoluwa
5. Oyedele Habibat
6. Abd'raheem Abd'rahman
7. Tijani Rahmat Morenikeji
8. Odunlami Faruq
9. Ettu-Ekindayo Monsurat
10. Ogunsola Mariam
11. Balogun Khadijah
12. Tijani Saheed
13. Lamidi Kafilat
14. John Fatiq
15. Olayanju Roqeebah
16. Abdul-Azeez Toheeb
17. Abdulsalam Muyibat
18. Adeniyi Sekinat
19. Busari Shukrah

www.ingramcontent.com/pod-product-compliance
Lightning Source LLC
Chambersburg PA
CBHW021150020426
42331CB00005B/980